J
599.3582

What's a
Lemming?

CREATURES ALL AROUND US

by D. M. Souza

 Carolrhoda Books, Inc./Minneapolis

Special thanks to Dr. R. Boonstra, Division of Life Sciences,
University of Toronto, Ontario, Canada, for helping with this book.

Carolrhoda Books, Inc., c/o The Lerner Publishing Group
241 First Avenue North, Minneapolis, MN 55401 U.S.A.

Website address: www.lernerbooks.com

Library of Congress Cataloging-in-Publication Data

Souza, D. M. (Dorothy M.)
    What's a lemming? / by D. M. Souza
        p.   cm. — (Creatures all around us)
    Includes index.
    Summary: Describes the life cycle, characteristics, and habitats of
lemmings.
    ISBN: 1-57505-088-9 (alk. paper)
    1. Lemmings—Juvenile literature. [1. Lemmings.] I. Title. II. Series:
Souza, D. M. (Dorothy M.). Creatures all around us.
QL737.R666S68 1998
599.35'82—dc21   97-36257

Manufactured in the United States of America
1 2 3 4 5 6 – JR – 03 02 01 00 99 98

What's a Lemming?

A lemming peeks out of its burrow in the snow.

It's icy cold across the land of the Far North. Birds have flown south and caribou, or reindeer, have found shelter and food in the forests. Winds howl, and now and then, cracking ice on frozen lakes and ponds sends up a boom. Moving around in tunnels beneath the snow are rugged little animals known as lemmings. They are one of the few kinds of creatures able to live in this place during the coldest months of the year.

3

But what exactly are lemmings? They are chubby, 5-inch-long **mammals.** Like all mammals, they have hair on their bodies and, when young, drink their mother's milk. Most lemmings weigh about 2 ounces, a little less than a candy bar.

Lemmings are mostly plant eaters.

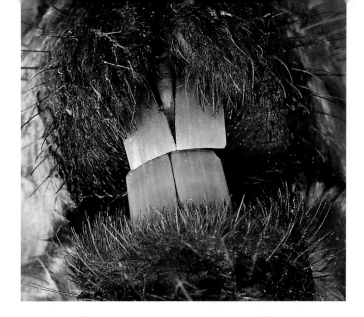

This beaver shows its incisors. Beavers are rodents and relatives of the lemming.

Because they have four large **incisors** (in-SY-zerz), or front teeth, lemmings are grouped with mammals known as **rodents.** Other rodents, such as mice, rats, squirrels, beavers, and porcupines, have large incisors, too. Most of these animals are **herbivores** (HER-buh-vorz), or plant eaters. They have the habit of gnawing, or chewing, on plants with their big front teeth.

Rodents' incisors grow the way our fingernails do, and the animals keep them trimmed by chewing on bark, the shells of seeds, or other hard objects. They also have from 12 to 24 **molars,** or grinding teeth, that help them break down their food. Lemmings have 6 molars in their upper jaw and 6 in their lower jaw.

Although lemmings are closely related to mice, they don't look much like them. A lemming's short tail, small eyes, and almost invisible ears make it look more like a hamster than a mouse.

The lemming's short tail and nearly hidden ears are less likely to freeze than if they were long and poked out.

Long, thick fur helps keep this collared lemming warm.

Lemmings have several ways of keeping themselves warm. When a freezing wind blows, the animals snuggle down inside long, thick, furry coats with their body heat trapped inside.

Some lemmings protect themselves from blasts of biting air by flattening their bodies close to the ground. Others have extra-long, stiff hairs that, like earmuffs, flip over and cover their ear openings. Many lemmings have fur even on the bottoms of their feet to protect them from the icy snow.

Most lemmings live on the icy **tundra**—huge, flat, almost treeless stretches of land—in northern Alaska, Canada, Europe, and Asia. Others hide in forests surrounding the tundra. Members of three groups of lemmings—the collared, the brown, and the bog lemming—can be found in North America. Some bog lemmings live as far south as the northern parts of the continental United States.

As we will see, all of these animals have fascinating ways of surviving, and every few years, some behave in rather unusual ways.

A collared lemming ventures out on the snowy tundra.

This collared lemming stays warm in its burrow in the snow.

Beneath the Snow

Inside a burrow, or tunnel, dug into the snow, a collared lemming snacks on the root of a plant. Above its burrow, cold winds blow across the snow. Inches beneath the burrow is **permafrost** (PER-muh-frahst), a layer of rock-hard, underground ice that never melts. In places, the permafrost is a mile thick. But inside the burrow, it's about 20 degrees warmer than it is above and below.

When it becomes too chilly, the lemming may plug the entrance of its burrow with snow and crawl inside a nest made of matted grass. This nest is like a warm sleeping bag, with the lemming snuggled inside.

9

The shields on the collared lemming's front feet help it to dig burrows in the snow.

If the lemming is hungry, it moves around its burrow searching for roots or other plants hidden in the snow. On the underside of the third and fourth toes of each of the collared lemming's front feet are big horny **shields,** or claws. These act like snow shovels and help the animal dig. When winter ends and there's no need to tunnel through the closely packed snow, the shields drop off. But before the next winter, they grow back again.

When it's not too cold, the collared lemming may dart outside to search for food. The collared lemming wears a coat of white fur in winter, which helps it hide from **predators,** animals that hunt and eat it. The white coat **camouflages** it, or makes the animal blend in with its surroundings—snow. The collared lemming is the only type of lemming that wears white in winter. In spring, the white hairs fall out and grayish brown ones take their place. A dark, thin stripe appears down its back, and golden hairs grow around its neck like a collar. That's why it's called a collared lemming.

Collared lemmings are the only type of lemmings that turn white in the winter.

Most of the time, lemmings live alone. But neighbors, some of whom may be brothers or sisters, live in burrows nearby. Lemmings spend their time digging and scurrying in and out of rooms in their snow house, where they nap, eat, and excrete, or go to the bathroom.

Some animals that live in cold climates, such as Arctic ground squirrels, grizzly bears, and Kodiak brown bears, hibernate (HY-bur-nayt), or fall into a deep sleep, during winter. They don't move around, and they don't eat. Instead, they live on fat stored in their bodies. But the collared lemming and its relatives do not hibernate. They stay busy year round.

A lemming's tracks through the snow

Spring and Summer Hideouts

This Arctic lemming's snow house is melting.

An Arctic lemming, a type of collared lemming, wakes from a nap and finds water dripping on its face and body. Water is falling like rain everywhere inside the burrow. Its snow house on the tundra is melting!

Each spring as the sun melts the snow, the lemming burrows collapse. Then the animals must find new hideouts above the permafrost.

Lemmings look for new homes in a variety of places. Some hide under or around stones and large rocks. Others look for soft patches of sandy soil or dry grasses where they can dig small burrows. Even after the big horny shields on their front toes fall off, lemmings can still dig with their strong front feet.

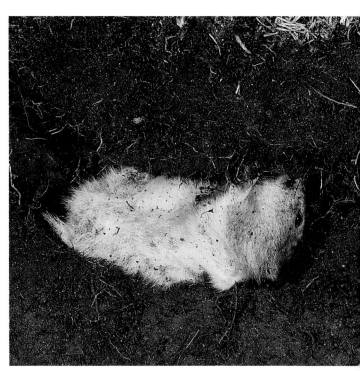

Left: *A nest and tunnels made by lemmings can be seen as snow melts.*
Right: *An Arctic lemming digs its way through soil to make a summer burrow.*

14

Sedges make a good hiding place for this brown lemming.

Soon sedges, or grasslike plants, begin to sprout on the tundra. These plants are small, because they cannot send deep roots into the frozen ground. But they grow close together and quickly form a thick carpet. Beneath this carpet, lemmings dig out new burrows or find old ones dug the year before. Some burrows may last two or more years.

The rodents use their incisors to clip grasses for soft beds and nests. They also line the passageways of their tunnels with plants for added warmth. Even though it's spring, the temperature outside is still very cold.

Each evening, when the sun is low in the sky, many lemmings poke their heads above ground, sniff the air, and listen for sounds of danger. Wild animals that left the area for winter are returning and looking for food. If the small rodents are not careful when they rush outside to nibble grasses, they may get stepped on by caribou or end up as some hungry creature's dinner.

Before long, the lemmings have eaten everything around them. Then they move on to another thick carpet of plants and find new things to eat and new places to hide.

This collared lemming must be on the lookout for predators as it snacks on tasty tundra plants.

Getting Together

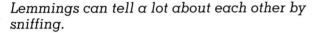

Lemmings can tell a lot about each other by sniffing.

Spring and summer are the times when male and female lemmings mate. They attract one another by giving off special **pheromones** (FAIR-uh-mohnz), or strong-smelling chemicals. Even though from a distance it may be hard for you to tell male and female lemmings apart, the animals have no trouble finding one another. They simply let their sharp sense of smell lead them to a mate.

After a few minutes of sniffing and licking, the male mounts, or climbs onto, the female's back. He then deposits **sperm**, or male cells, inside her. Some of his sperm join with her eggs and start to grow into tiny developing lemmings.

17

Once they've mated, females build special nests for their soon-to-be-born young. The nests are made of shredded plant stems and lined with soft mosses.

Pregnant lemmings quickly grow fat and wide. Some brown lemmings become so wide they end up looking more like pears than rodents. They may even have to enlarge their burrows so they can move from place to place.

Clipped grass makes a cozy nest for this Greenland collared lemming.

These brown lemmings are two to three days old. They are not much bigger than a dime.

In about 20 days, a **litter,** or group of babies, is born. An average litter of lemmings has three to seven blind, furless **pups,** or babies.

Almost immediately, the pups begin sipping warm milk from their mother's teats, or nipples. The mother lemming watches closely over her pups. She keeps them warm by tucking them deep inside the nesting material or covering them with the warmth of her body. Sometimes the warmth from this bundle sends up enough heat to melt some of the spring snow that may fall on the burrow.

Sleeping collared lemming pups keep each other warm.

Baby lemmings learn to know their mother by her scent. The pups' eyes don't open until about 11 days after they are born, so their noses must tell them when their mother or a stranger comes near. Their mother spends a lot of time licking and cleaning them. As the pups' fur grows in, this constant licking gives their new coats a silky shine.

Lower incisors begin to appear in the tiny mouths after about six days, and a day later the upper ones break through the gums. Soon the young are able to sample foods other than milk.

In less than a month's time, the young look very much like grown-up lemmings. At this point, they have learned all they need to know in order to survive, so they leave the nest to search for burrows of their own. Soon they will begin raising new families.

Females are often only three weeks old and males only a month old when they first mate. Females usually have two litters each year. But some years they have many more.

A mother collared lemming protects her young.

Too Many Lemmings

The Norway lemming is a type of brown lemming.

A female brown lemming, also known as a true lemming, is licking her 6 new pups. They are fat and healthy because this year more plants than usual have sprouted on the tundra. For some reason, perhaps because of all the food, the female will soon mate again and raise several more litters. Instead of having 6 pups in each litter, she may have as many as 11.

Nearby, other brown lemmings are also having more babies—and not just 2 litters, but 4 or more. Soon, in places where 20 lemmings normally live, 120 are crowded together. There is not even enough space to dig new burrows.

22

Males begin bumping into young males, getting into boxing matches with them, and trying to drive them away. Females have a hard time finding places to hide their nests. Young lemmings from one family run in and out of the burrows of other families. Food soon becomes so scarce that many of the rodents must leave to find fresh patches of delicious plants.

A Norway lemming looks for food.

Norway lemmings must look for new homes when their old ones get too crowded.

   Some of the lemmings set out, one by one, to find other places to live. They emigrate, or leave their homes, never to return again. Along the way, they are joined by other brown lemmings doing the same thing. Hundreds of the furry brown animals are scurrying over the ground. They squeak, bark, and whistle as they call to one another, greet newcomers, or warn others that predators are near. Sometimes they snack on so many grasses, mosses, or plants in people's gardens that they leave bare patches of land along the way.

If a lake, pond, or river lies across their path, the animals don't change direction or try to move around the water. They plunge in and begin paddling. Some drown in the crush of bodies. Others are snapped up by hungry fish. Those that reach the other side shake themselves like puppies and continue their search.

Once in a while, the animals reach the edge of the open sea. To them, it looks like just another lake, pond, or river, so they jump in. But with no shoreline ahead, they soon tire and drown.

People in Norway who have seen large numbers of lemmings jumping into the sea have wondered what they were doing. The animals were simply looking for new homes that were surrounded by good things to eat.

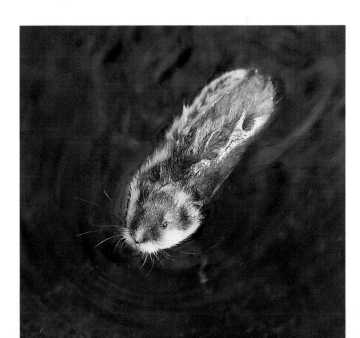

Lemmings will swim across water if they need to.

Other types of rodents also have more pups than normal during some years. But during the year following the growth in population, these rodents usually have fewer babies. This rise and fall in numbers is called a **cycle,** and it usually takes place every three to five years.

Scientists are not certain what causes these cycles. Some think it may be due to predators. Others believe the amount or kind of food may affect the animals. Still others suspect that changes within the animals themselves may bring about the cycles. Whatever the cause, no rodents increase in numbers quite like the brown lemmings do, especially those known as Norway lemmings.

In some years, collared lemmings have larger families than usual. Then, like Norway lemmings, they must move to homes where they can find enough food.

In a Cold Bog

This bog in New Hampshire is home to bog lemmings.

A thick carpet of mosses and decayed plants, known as a **bog,** stretches over the edge of a pond. Each year, the carpet grows thicker and, like a giant sponge, it soaks up more and more water. Because no sunlight shines beneath the bog, the water is ice cold. Plants grow on top of the carpet and people can walk on it, but when they do, the carpet jiggles like a waterbed. Many bogs in Canada and the cold northern parts of the United States are home to bog lemmings.

Bog lemmings are cinnamon brown with touches of gray, yellow, and black on the upper parts of their bodies. Their underparts are usually grayish white.

In spring and summer, bog lemmings dig out burrows 6 to 12 inches below the surface of the moss carpet. The animals do not dig any deeper than this because it's too damp and cold farther down. In their underground burrows, they set up rooms for sleeping, eating, storing food for winter, and raising their young.

Every now and then, the lemmings run along above-ground pathways. They jog so often that plants become matted down by their tracks. Along the way, they clip different snacks with their sharp front teeth and return to their tunnels through any one of a number of entrances. Their favorite foods are grasses, roots, and stems. Once in a while, they may even eat slugs, snails, and insects.

A southern bog lemming looks for food.

Beginning in March, three to seven bog lemming pups usually appear in nests lined with plants, bits of fur, and even feathers. The nests may be hidden under stumps, inside hollow logs, or within burrows. The young remain with their mother until she is almost ready to give birth to another litter. Then they leave to dig homes of their own.

Like their relatives in the Far North, bog lemmings don't hibernate during winter. They dig tunnels in the snow, munch on food they stored during summer and fall, take short naps, and watch for predators.

Bog lemmings, like this southern bog lemming, stay active all year round.

Enemies

A brown lemming peeks out from its hiding place.

Many animals, especially in the Arctic, depend on lemmings for food. The rodents must be constantly on the lookout for these predators. During summer, lemmings cannot hide under cover of darkness, because there is little or no night in the Arctic at this time of year. For weeks at a time, the sun may shine for 24 hours.

This Arctic fox has caught a lemming for lunch.

One of the predators lemmings must look out for is the fox. Foxes often sniff the ground, searching for the scent of lemmings. If a fox finds a lemming snacking on grasses, it pounces on the rodent, holds it under its front paws for a few minutes, then snaps it up into its jaws and carries it home.

In years when many lemmings are born, female foxes may have more young than usual. Fox pups are then fed a steady diet of the rodents. One family of foxes may eat hundreds of lemmings before moving out of its den, or hideout, for the season. When winter comes and the rodents hide under the snow, many foxes must move south to search for other things to eat.

Male snowy owls, birds that live on the tundra, not only eat lemmings, they also bring them as gifts to females they want to win as mates. A male will swoop down, catch a rodent by the back of its neck, and bring it to the female. He will do the same thing several times a day for almost a week, or until the female agrees to mate.

Scientists have discovered that the number of eggs a female snowy owl lays often depends on the number of lemmings she has been given. If she has received many, she may lay close to 10 eggs. But if lemmings are scarce and the male can find only a few, the female snowy owl may not even build a nest.

Each day snowy owls catch many lemmings for their young to eat.

Gulls, ravens, hawks, and sea birds known as jaegers also hunt lemmings. Sometimes caribou will chase the creatures and catch them under their hoofs. Even bears may snatch one or two lemmings if they cross their paths.

Weasels, however, are the most dangerous predators of all. They often follow lemmings into their burrows and try to take over their hideouts and their nests. Lemmings don't give up easily, though. When attacked, a lemming will stand on its hind legs, face the predator, and struggle to defend itself.

If a lemming is out of its burrow and spots an enemy before its neighbors do, it will whistle or squeal a warning to the others. Then each one dashes back into its burrow. With so many predators hunting them, it's surprising that these tiny creatures ever become as numerous as they do.

With claws up and teeth bared, this collared lemming is prepared to defend itself.

Like mice, lemmings play an important role in the environment. As we have seen, they provide food for animals that often can find little else to eat. In spring, their diggings let the rays of the sun shine closer to the permafrost and melt part of it. Their droppings nourish the soil so that many different plants can grow. Whether they live on the icy tundra, in damp meadows and forests, or in cold bogs, these hearty little rodents have learned to survive and multiply where few other animals can.

A collared lemming sits in its summertime burrow.

Lemmings belong to a group of mammals known as rodents. The group includes animals such as mice, rats, squirrels, beavers, and porcupines. Some scientists place lemmings in the same family as deer mice. Others place them in the family with the house mouse. Below are the scientific names of three kinds of lemmings, various members of each group, and a few facts about them.

GENUS	EXAMPLES	SIZE IN INCHES	FAVORITE FOODS	HABITAT
Dicrostonyx	collared lemmings: Arctic Greenland Hudson Bay	4¾–6	grasses, roots, bulbs	tundra in Greenland, Arctic islands, Quebec, Alaska, Siberia
Lemmus	brown lemmings: black-footed Norway	4½–5½	grasses, roots, bulbs	tundra or forests in Scandinavia and on islands near Alaska
Synaptomys	bog lemmings: northern southern	3½–4¾	mosses, insects, slugs	bogs, swamps, meadows in Canada, Alaska, northern United States

Glossary

bog: spongy ground made up of mosses and other plants growing tightly together

camouflage: to blend in with one's surroundings

cycle: a rise and fall in the population of some animals

herbivore: a plant-eating animal

incisors: the four front teeth of some animals

litter: the group of young that are born to an animal at one time

mammals: animals that have hair on most of their bodies and feed their young with mother's milk

molars: broad, flat teeth on either side of an animal's mouth that are used for grinding and chewing food

permafrost: in the tundra, the soil a few inches underground that is always frozen

pheromones: strong-smelling chemicals that animals give off during mating season

predators: animals that hunt and eat other animals

pups: the young of certain animals, such as lemmings and foxes

rodent: an animal, such as a mouse or a lemming, with four large front teeth

shields: large claws, on two toes of each of a collared lemming's front feet, that help the animal dig through closely packed snow

sperm: male cells that fertilize a female's eggs

tundra: the flat, almost treeless land in northern Alaska, Canada, Europe, and Asia

Index

The photographs are reproduced through the courtesy of: Natural History
Photographic Agency: (© Paal Hermansen) cover, pp. 22, 24, (© Hellio & Van Ingen)
back cover, p. 33, (© Alan Williams) pp. 1 (right), 16, (© Stephen Krasemann) p. 5;
Canadian Museum of Nature: (© S.D. MacDonald) pp. 3, 11, (© Martin Lipman)
p. 17; Peter Arnold, Inc.: (© Klein/Hubert/Bios) pp. 4, 37, (Bios) p. 23, (© Marielle
Bruno/Bios) p. 25; © Michael Durham/ENP Images, p. 6; The National Audubon
Society/Photo Researchers: (© Tom & Pat Leeson) pp. 1 (left), 31, (© Tom McHugh)
pp. 7, 10, 15, 18, 20, 21, 35, (© Jim Cartier) p. 26, (© Stephen Krasemann) p. 32;
Mammal Slide Library: (© R. Riewe) p. 8, (L.L. Master) p. 29; © J.L. Klein & M.L.
Hubert, pp. 9, 13, 14 (right); © David A. Gill, pp. 12, 14 (left); Jamie Barger/University
of Alaska-Fairbanks, p. 19; Karlene Schwartz, p. 27; © Roger W. Barbour, p. 30.